KZ & MK, Better Than Ever

The True Story of the Mystic Lakes Bald Eagles Continues

By John Harrison & Kim Nagy

Also by John Harrison and Kim Nagy

Dead In Good Company:
A Celebration of Mount Auburn Cemetery

True Wildlife Adventure Series for Children

Skylar's Great Adventure
The True Story of a Brave Fresh Pond Owlet

Star Guy's Great Adventure
The True Story of a Salisbury Snowy Owl

Big Caesar's New Home
The True Story of a Coyote Season at Mount Auburn Cemetery

Wally & Wind of the Woburn Cliffs
The True Story of a Peregrine Falcon Family

KZ and MK, Lord and Lady of the Lakes
A True Story of the Mystic Lakes Bald Eagles

Ziggy Owl Press

ISBN-13: 978-0-9963747-9-8

“We're waiting for the chirp, chirp, chirp of an eaglet being born.”

"The Egg" by Sherman Edwards, from the Tony-Award winning musical 1776

Dedication

KZ & MK is dedicated to the next generation of Bald Eagle kids.

Oscar Kinsman, Sammy Kinsman, Simone Cruz, Quinn Hadley Paulson, Talya Feldman, Ilana Feldman, Henry Elias Maier, Sam Hursh, Will Hursh, Lucy Shanfeld, Jesse Carrier Jr., Isabella Carrier, Rose Aryss Hamel, Ella Malvey, Sophia Charlotte Breakstone, Benjamin French, Mason George Drudi, Jack Travis Drudi, Oaklyn Elizabeth Drudi, Layla Nathan, Tennessee Tuttle, Wallis Tuttle, Ella Higginson, Lucille Higginson, Madelyn Roussell, Patrick Roussell, Colin Roussell, Donovan Roussell, Bernadette Roussell, Sophia Matthews, Olivia Matthews, Violet Matthews, Ophelia Matthews, Saoirse Matthews, Canyon Tallman, Carrigan Tallman, Corby Scott Cunningham, Camry Cunningham, Cyler Cunningham, Abigail Parker, Oliver Woolverton Barnett, Olivia Wlodarczyk, Audrey Bradley, Addison Bradley, Amelia Bradley, Nel Rabens, Nora Rabens, Nathaniel Nearhood, Caitlin Gower, Nora Gower, Grace Gower, Katherine Rita Sullivan, Cheng-Loong, Cheng-Lin, Saddie Lesso, Adria Hadidian, Eliace Hadidian, Ellieah Marabella, Benjamin Marabella, Joshua Marabella, Francis Santarpio, Haidyn Santarpio, Willa Alford, Josie Alford, Harrison Balakier, Kenzie DeCoste, Olivia DiBari, Leo Gallagher, Lydia Harris, Ella Karp, Nola M., Everett O'Brien, Axcie Pucko, Lailah Rockwell, Arden Treadwell, Noah Welch, Layla Bryan, Ella Bryan, Carter Bryan, Jordan Brennan, John Connors, Thomas Anderson, Riley Shay Doss, Maddie Lee Dahlbeck, Wyatt Dahlbeck, Grace

Hanafin, Charlie Hanafin, Dylan Simard, Levi Simard, Celine Shedd, Remy Shedd, Elijah Shapiro, Joshua Shapiro, Silvio Ortiz, Brayden Campbell, Jackson Campbell, Bennett Zalinski, Colin Zalinski, August Zalinski, Declan Haley, Thomas Haley, Shay Shay, Nora Whalen, Brian Whalen, Henry Duval, John Duval, Zayah Asher Perlmutter, Caleb Jack Perlmutter, Mila Sage Perlmutter, Zachary Michael Kaplan, Cameron James Kaplan, Hannah Baron Silva, Ty Minogue, Kaelyn Minogue, Spencer Minogue, Nell Madigan Minogue, Eliana Minogue, Declan Minogue, Hazel Leslie, Lydia Leslie, Justin Williamson, Zinnia Lili Roehl-Gordon, Lamine Gordon, Madeline Rhunette Aandahl, Spencer David Aandahl, Bernadine DeMatteo, Annetta DeMatteo, Maggie Carey, Hugh Carey III, Annie Carey, Patrick O'Neill, Emma O'Neill, Danny O'Neill, Molly O'Neil, Addison Hale, Isobel Hale, Brooks Camorali, Nathan Robert Gaskill, Pierce Edward Antonsen, Cooper Mack Antonsen, Quinlan Grace Hagan, Shea Alice Hagan, Ryann Rose Hagan, Miles Hagan, Aurora Krueger, Ryanna Krueger, Parker Donahue, Jaxsen Daniel, Antonio Strate, Jack Sorrentino, Max Sorrentino, Mary Abigail McElwreath, Caroline Marguerite McElwreath, Evelyn Rose Riggs, Corinne Grace Riggs, Norah Lynn Riggs, Hailey Rene Riggs, Rhea Coogan, Della Coogan, Adrian Vogel, Sage Vogel, Oliver Vogel, Emma Vogel, Bailey Rose Sherman, Vivienne Sophia Sherman, Rose Charlotte Baker, Madeline DiGiorgio, Amelia DiGiorgio, Jocelyn Gesner, Ian Gesner, Evelyn Lamer, Owen Lamer, Ivan Lakits, Camille Horstman, Chesney Schlereth, Violet Nina, Noah Allen, Jude Allen and the grandchildren of the Boston Admirals Club employees.

MK, a female Bald Eagle, sat quietly on her nest, waiting. It was early March. She was incubating eggs, to keep them warm. It would take about a month for her eggs to hatch. The late winter days ticked away, and soon it would be spring.

This was an exciting time. Everything was new. MK and KZ, her mate, had a new home, not far from their old nest at the Mystic Lakes. They had found an old Red-tailed Hawk nest in a nearby cemetery, and added to it to accommodate their future family.

Throughout the winter, they had worked hard building their new home, and we watched it get bigger every day. In addition to branches, the eagles also searched for moss, grass and twigs to take back to the nest. These would act like soft carpeting for the eggs.

Last year, even though they were not fully mature, MK & KZ built a nest and tried to have a family. A male Bald Eagle from New York attempted to drive KZ from MK and their nest, but KZ prevailed. There were many threats last year, and they were unsuccessful in having a family.

But they had learned a lot. All the past challenges made the bond between them stronger. Now they were more mature, and they tried again.

On April 8, the first eaglet hatched! We could tell there was a baby, because MK's behavior changed. We didn't know how many other eggs, if any, MK was incubating. We wouldn't see the eaglet for several weeks, because it had to get strong enough to stand up in the nest for us to see it, but it was exciting nevertheless.

It was a good day to be born!

3 WEEKS

All the watchers and photographers were so happy for MK & KZ. The eagles had had such a hard time last year. KZ ended up fighting off several male Bald Eagles who were interested in MK, and their nest at the Mystic Lakes. But this pair persevered, and they finally succeeded. They never gave up.

April 08, 2021
KZ is a dad!

Almost three weeks later, we saw the first eaglet struggle to stand up in the nest! The eaglet was covered with soft white down, and many times a day we could see its head from where we were watching, far below. Soon a second head appeared, and now the eaglet had a sibling.

MK and KZ had a family!

KZ, a first-time father, now had two eaglets to feed. He was very busy, because the eaglets were always hungry. Fish are the primary food for eagles, and there were plenty of fish in the Mystic Lakes. KZ liked to perch on "The Tree," above the spillway at the dam, where he could catch fish to take back to MK and the eaglets.

"THE TREE"
MEDFORD BOAT CLUB
SPILLWAY

KZ delivered the fish to MK, and she fed the eaglets. Sometimes KZ fed the eaglets, but usually it was MK, their mother, who fed them.

4 WEEKS

The nest was very active and the eaglets were getting bigger and bigger. As they grew larger, we could see more of them when they stood up in the nest. They lost their white baby down, and their first feathers came in brown-flecked with white. At five weeks, they were large enough to be nearly fully visible to us.

When the eaglets were six weeks old, we knew it would soon be time for them to be banded. Bands are identifying rings on their legs, with letters and numbers. These bands would help us learn about the eaglets and where they traveled after they left the nest.

6 WEEKS

5 WEEKS

7 WEEKS

We weren't sure if the pine tree that held the eagle nest was safe enough for a climber, though. It was crooked and heavily limbed. MassWildlife would determine if it was safe enough to climb.

On Wednesday, May 19, the MassWildlife crew arrived. MK and KZ knew something was up. They flew around, agitated, calling to the eaglets. A rope had already been sent up near the nest, secured on a limb. We could see both eaglets in the nest as we waited below. The parents communicated to the eaglets, and the eaglets dropped down deep in the nest to hide. We didn't see them for a while.

After an hour of inspecting, the MassWildlife crew decided that the pine tree was safe to climb, and Jesse Caney, one of the primary climbers, organized his gear, and then began the long climb up.

It took about thirty minutes for Jesse to reach the top. He carried a canvas bag in which to put one eaglet, and a wooden stick with a metal ring to draw the eaglet to the edge of the nest so he could safely collect it and put it in the bag.

When Jesse was approaching the nest, curiosity got the better of the eaglets, and they stood at the edge of the nest, looking down at Jesse's orange helmet. What did they think of that, we wondered!

When Jesse was eye level with the eaglets, they retreated to the back of the nest, frightened. Jesse took out his wooden stick and pulled one eaglet toward him. Gently he gathered the bird, and put it in the canvas bag. The bag was lowered by a pulley, and Dave Paulson, MassWildlife Senior Endangered Species Review Biologist, waited below. He reached up, secured the eaglet, and brought it over to the waiting banding crew. An excited audience watched the eaglets being banded.

The eaglet was healthy and robust. Because everyone was quiet and calm, the eaglet seemed more curious than afraid. The crew affixed an identifying band to the eaglet, 25C, which they thought was a female. After measurements and an inspection, the eaglet was placed in the bag and returned to the nest, where Jesse waited patiently.

FIRM GRIP

Then Jesse got the second eaglet into the bag, and repeated the process. Meanwhile, MK was flying around, still agitated. We felt sorry for her, and wondered if she remembered her own banding, many years before.

The second eaglet, thought to be a male, was also healthy and strong. He was banded with band 26C. After the same measurements and inspection, the eaglet was put in the bag and returned to the nest. We were so happy and relieved that we clapped! In a short while, MK finally ended her frantic flying, and returned to the nest.

26
C

Life returned to normal, and the eaglets settled down to start some serious and rapid growth, because in about a month, they would be branching. This means they would walk out of the nest, hold on tight to the tree limbs, and flap their wings hard and fast. It would give them the strength and stamina they would need for their first flight – the most important day in their lives.

MASSWILDLIFE

As the eaglets grew, KZ and MK spent more time away from the nest. This was necessary to make the eaglets independent – and ultimately to make them want to leave the nest for good. The parents might have been away from the nest, but they were never far away. They were always close by watching and protecting their family.

It was fun to watch the eagle family, and sometimes they did funny things. Once KZ landed on the seat of a boat at the Medford Boat Club. Facing forward, he looked as if he was the Captain about to motor away! Sometimes small birds followed KZ and MK.

One morning MK took off from a favorite tree at the Lakes with an Eastern Kingbird on her back! Was she trying to be an Uber Flyer? Another time she flew above us, trailing long sheets of toilet paper! And sometimes one of them would try to take off with branches too big to carry away.

Watching these eaglets reminded us that MK, their mother, was hatched only a few miles away in nearby Waltham. Five years ago, MK looked just like her two kids!

MK 2016

The summer progressed, and so did the eaglets. They began to branch and to move around on the tree limbs. To us watching below, it looked like they were planning their first flight, trying out nearby branches and hoping to find the right one for the right day.

Early in the morning of June 30, 25C launched high, left the branch behind, and became airborne! 25C flew above us in circles. Then she flew to a nearby tree, and landed well. Flying was fun! After resting a bit, she took off, and continued to practice.

25C Fledge Morning
June 30, 2021
8:30am

On July 1, 26C fledged! They were 83 and 84 days old, respectively. The eaglets were now officially fledglings. For the rest of the summer and into the fall, they would learn how to become eagles, both from their parents, and from their natural, innate eagle instincts that they were born with.

There was much to learn - like how to hunt and fish. It would take time to build this important skill set. For now, the parents would catch prey, and take it to the nest. The eaglets were very food motivated! No matter where they were in the cemetery, they always would quickly return to the nest for a meal!

One morning, 25C was being harassed by a loud and irritating Blue Jay. Many raptors are harassed by Blue Jays, crows and other birds. This particular Blue Jay followed 25C from the roof of a house to a spruce tree, buzzing close and shrieking loudly. But then MK brought in a fish and 25C was "saved!" Time for breakfast!

25C was a bold and strong flyer, right from the beginning. One morning, she flew over the trees toward the Mystic Lakes. We thought the fledgling would circle around, and return, but she did not. We knew that one day soon, both eaglets would range out into the world, look for their own territories to call home, and begin their own life adventure.

We hoped that KZ and MK would continue to live in the cemetery and raise more eaglets. We were grateful that the eagle population was growing, so that we could continue to witness the miracle of life as our country's symbol thrived and persevered, against all odds.

MK & KZ – A History, Susan Moses

MK was hatched during the week of April 10, 2016 at Mt. Feake Cemetery in Waltham, MA. She was banded there on May 25. MK fledged on or about July 10, 2016.

MK was last seen around her nest area in Waltham on September 10, 2016.

Her next reported sighting was at the Mystic Lakes Dam on September 26, 2016 before she headed south. On October 16, 2016 MK was seen in NJ (Burlington County).

She found her way to NY (Dutchess County - Wappingers Falls in Wappingers Creek and the Hudson River) for a few weeks around January 30, 2017.

On April 2, 2017 MK was spotted back at Mt. Feake. Her parents were there but no new kids yet (this is the year the first nest - where MK grew up - fell and her parents had to rebuild in another tree - where the current nest is). She has been spotted at Mt. Feake a couple of times since then.

She was at the Mystic Lakes in early November 2018 and on November 9 was spotted at Claypit Pond in Belmont and hung out there for awhile.

Around the same time (November 2018) she also hung out around Blair Pond in Cambridge, MA and visited Fresh Pond too.

It is thought that MK and KZ have been together at the Mystic Lakes since 2019.

KZ was banded on June 22, 2015 after being found on the ground under the nest the day before. He was taken to the Tufts Wildlife Clinic for a possible wing injury, but found to be in good health.

He was released below the nest on Little Island in Webster Lake, Webster, MA. KZ was believed to be a male based on his small size.

It is thought that KZ was first seen at the Mystic Lakes some time after March 2019 (which was when MK was hanging out with an older eagle, 9E).

MK as a fledgling - 2016

ACKNOWLEDGMENTS

We give special thanks to our first readers: Bobbie Gatz, Dr. Mariana Castells, Sharon Sherman, Corinne & Artty Kinsman, Don and Geri Tremblay, Ursula and Dave Goodine, Cyn McCarthy & Laura and Steve Duggan.

Our gratitude for Peter Filichia, Linda Konner, Ray Cilley, Upton Bell, JoAnne O'Neill, Paul Treseler, Paul Roberts, Bob and Edie Di Giorgio, James Harrison, Mary Hogan, Joe Plati, Joe and Karen Polvere, Keith and Cathy Joyce, Bob and Becky Parsons, Mark Nickerson, Craig Gibson, Ray Brown of Talkin' Birds, Gary Goshgarian, Jeanne Bohen, William Martin, Cathy and Dick Minogue, Frank and Bobbie Gatz, John Amaral, Sangeet Kaur Khalsa, Dawna Blum of Wild Birds Unlimited, our Wildlife Whisperer John Sullivan and - always - Steve Gladstone, who brings ideas and manuscripts to life.

Thank you Michael Armanious, Jeff Munro, Katie Chang, Jonathan Barbato, Norm McLeod and the staff of Arlington Community Media for your continuing support and for making our Dead In Good Company video, Skylar's Great Adventure videos and the continuing Conversations With Creative Minds video series.

Special thanks to the MassWildlife crew that banded 25C and 26C: Dave Paulson, Chalis Bird, Tim Mathews, Derek McDermott, Josh Gahagan, Jesse Caney, Anne Gagnon and Leslie Gabrilska.

A shout out to Mike O'Connell who witnessed the first fledge ever of a Mystic Lakes eaglet, 25C, around 5am on June 30, 2021. Mike witnessed a moment in history!

And a shout-out to Sue McClelland, one of our keen eagle observer-spotters.

We thank Diane Welch, Arlington's Award-Winning Animal Control Officer, for her tireless efforts with our eaglet 26C.

And lastly, in loving memory of our friends in wildlife - Ernie Sarro, Virginia Parsons, Deb Cilley and Frank T. Peace, Sr.

ABOUT THE AUTHORS

John Harrison and Kim Nagy are the Editors of ***Dead in Good Company,*** a compelling collection of essays, poems and wildlife photographs of Mount Auburn Cemetery in Cambridge, Massachusetts. Sweet Auburn, as it's affectionately known, is America's first garden cemetery, and ***Dead in Good Company*** is the first book to celebrate the Cemetery as a place of regeneration and transformation; the circle of life. Mount Auburn Cemetery is one of New England's Birding Hotspots.

The True Wildlife Adventure Series includes ***Skylar's Great Adventure: The True Story of a Brave Fresh Pond Owlet, Star Guy's Great Adventure: The True Story of a Salisbury Snowy Owl, Big Caesar's New Home: The True Story of a Coyote Season at Mount Auburn Cemetery, Wally & Wind of the Woburn Cliffs: The True Story of a Peregrine Falcon Family,*** and ***KZ & MK, Lord and Lady of the Lakes: A True Story of the Mystic Lakes Bald Eagles.***

See more at: www.facebook.com/deadingoodcompany

John Harrison founded Epilog Enterprises, a book distribution company, in 1975. His passion for nature ultimately led to the idea for this book. His photographs have been published by Mass Audubon, the Humane Society of the United States, and Project Coyote in CA, and have appeared in books, calendars, magazines, newspapers, and websites. He lectures on nature and wildlife at elementary schools and to senior citizen groups. Additionally, he authored the *Medford Wildlife Watch* blog for The Medford Transcript newspaper for ten years.

Kim Nagy has made the natural world both her profession and her hobby. She is an avid wildlife and nature photographer, and travels widely in pursuit of her craft. She works as a National Sales Manager in the natural products industry. Her photos have appeared in National Geographic's Daily Dozen, *BirdWatching, The BirdNote* calendar, several publications of the Massachusetts Audubon Society, *The Marco Review,* Tin Mountain Conservation Center, *Monadnock Table*, The Harris Center for Conservation and on the Java Planet Organic Coffee Company website (photo by Ryan Butler).

See more at: www.facebook.com/catchlightphotos

PHOTO CREDITS

- John Harrison: Front Cover, 3, 7, 11, 21, 27, 28, 29, 31, 39, 43, 49, 59, 67, 75, 85, 91, 100
- Kim Nagy: Back Cover, 33, 41, 45, 47, 51, 53, 55, 57, 58, 78, 101
- Patty Sears-Joyce: 9, 37
- Phil Sorrentino: 13
- Jay Richard: 15
- Rick Olick: 17
- Jim Joyce: 19, 36
- Anna Piccolo: 23
- Andy Kawa: 25
- Nancy Gower: 35
- Bobby Richards: 61
- Charles Tse: 63
- Chih-Chen Tse: 64
- Guilong Charles Cheng: 65
- Rene Meuse: 68
- Jim Renault: 69, 96
- Scott Creamer: 71
- Kathy Valone: 73
- Steve Giurlando: 77
- Angelika O'Connor: 79
- Paul Treseler: 81
- Maureen Begin: 82
- Shaikh Rajibul Hoque: 83
- Howard Muscott: 87
- Rich Turk: 89
- Paul Roberts: 90
- Susan Moses: 93, 94, 95
- Photo conversion to illustration by Steve Gladstone

Fledgling 25C

Fledgling 26C

Made in the USA
Middletown, DE
15 September 2021